Typeset by Avon Dataset Ltd, Bidford-on-Avon, Warks

Printed and bound in Great Britain by
The Guernsey Press Co. Ltd, Channel Islands

Hodder Children's Books
a division of Hodder Headline plc
338 Euston Road
London NW1 3BH

HEROIC HORSES

Sue Welford

Illustrated by
Trevor Newton

Hodder
Children's
Books

A division of Hodder Headline plc

Acknowledgements

Thanks to the following for their
help in researching this book:

Ashford Library
The International Museum of the
    Horse
Museum of Victoria, Australia
Misty of Chincoteague
    Foundation, Virginia, USA
St Ives Museum
The St Ives Times and Echo
Mr Ted Rowe
Lesley Pollinger

Contents

SEFTON
the Miracle Horse

It was the 'Swingin' Sixties' when a horse breeder in Southern Ireland sold a young black colt with a white blaze and four white socks to a dealer buying horses to sell to the British army. At that time, the colt didn't have a name. The dealer didn't really know why he chose that particular animal. Maybe it was his cheeky personality, or the energy that made him dance and buck as he felt the wind through his long mane and tail. Maybe it was that vitality the dealer could see in his eyes. Whatever it was, the man had a good eye and knew that his high spirits were a sign of intelligence and courage. What he didn't know, though, was that this particular young horse would come to depend upon that spirit and courage for his very survival.

For the first four years of his life, the young animal grazed the green pastures of Ireland, south west of Waterford, where he shared his meadow with twenty or so other youngsters. There, they put on muscle and grew strong, sturdy and independent. They didn't see many people, only the dealer now and then who would come to check their welfare with a tit-bit or two in his pocket. This young horse was always the first to prick up his ears at strange sounds or to flare his nostrils into the wind for unusual smells. He was alert and strong, swift on his feet and ready for anything. His owner knew he would soon be ready to join the army.

One summer day, three army officers arrived to inspect the young stock. Our horse was paraded in front of them. One of the men examined him. Ears, eyes, teeth, sturdy limbs. They all commented on his spirit, his strength of character. Soon the deal was done and the colt's life changed dramatically when he was brought to England by boat to begin his army career.

His first home was the Household Cavalry barracks next to Buckingham Palace. He was given a number, 5816, and later a name, Sefton, a name that years afterwards was to be on everyone's lips. From then on, he was destined to have an interesting and varied career.

From the very beginning, Sefton turned out to be a bit of a rebel. He had been taken to Wellington Barracks for six months' basic education and this was where the next stage of his career would be decided. Number 5816, as he was still, at that time, known, showed that he could be very naughty and strong-willed when the mood took him. He didn't respond so willingly as some of the other young horses. He wanted to trot, not walk, he wanted to canter, not trot. He showed he had a fiery spirit. His trainers knew though, that once they had the animal's confidence he would make a splendid cavalry horse.

But it seemed Sefton had other ideas. When the horses faced their final test at the end of their six months' training, a parade past a group of bandsmen in full swing, Sefton pranced and reared and snorted at the horrible din. To his trainers' great disappointment, he failed to qualify as a troop horse. Where other horses might have been discarded, though, Sefton was given another chance and allowed to take part in a very important event, The Queen's Birthday Parade. A great honour indeed for a horse who had yet to prove himself.

By now, Sefton was fully grown. He was a beautiful animal, his white blaze and socks a brilliant contrast to the sheen of his coal black coat.

At the Birthday Parade it was obvious to everyone that Sefton was, at heart, still the spirited youngster he had been in the fields of Ireland, and to his rider's horror as the Queen rode out to inspect her Guards, Sefton decided he'd had enough of standing still. He hated the noise of the crowds, the bands, the flags. He decided he would not walk sedately like the other horses, he would trot, canter and even do a little sideways dance. No horse of the honourable Household Cavalry should ever behave like this!

As a result of this incident Sefton received still more training in the manner and ways of a dignified member of the army. Everyone loved his strength of character and they were determined he would finally make the grade.

Three months later he entered the riding school once more to face the bandsmen at the pass out parade. His trainers held their breath. Would Sefton pass muster this time? If not they were very much afraid he would have to be sold.

This time, Sefton behaved himself. Everyone was overjoyed. At last the young horse had become a fully qualified member of the Royal

Horse Guards Troop. All their hard work had paid off in the end. Sefton had arrived!

But Sefton was to disgrace himself once more as a ceremonial horse. He was soon up to his old spirited tricks again. It seemed his run of good luck was over when he managed to unseat a corporal of the horse troop and leave him sprawling on the ground. For the time being at least, Sefton's ceremonial days were over.

After that he spent some years away from London, training young army riders, taking part in hunter trials. He even became a brilliant and fearless showjumper. He had already earned a reputation for being willing and steadfast at every task he undertook. Everyone who cared for him loved his good humour, his kindness and his sometimes naughty behaviour. He was a great showman and loved attention. One of his favourite tricks was to grab his bridle off its stable hook and throw it on the floor. For the soldier whose time was dedicated to the smartness of the horses, this was a real test of patience.

After a stint in Germany Sefton came back to London. He already belonged to the Blues and Royals and was destined to be a member of a new regiment of the Household Cavalry. Residents and visitors to London would often stop to watch as Sefton and his companions and their riders came trotting smartly round Hyde Park Corner, their spotless harnesses jangling, their proud heads tossing, their coats shining in the early morning sun. Nobody knew that it would be on this spot, many years later, that one of the greatest horrors of army history would take place.

It was a peaceful, sunny summer morning when Sefton set out on his ceremonial walk to the Horse Guards. He was now one of the oldest horses in the parade. He looked in tip-top condition. His black coat gleamed in the sunshine, his white socks and blaze were the colour of snow, his hooves were oiled and shining. He felt great. Proud to be a member of the Queen's Horse Guard and eager to please his rider, Trooper Michael Pedersen. By now, Sefton was every inch the best horse in the barracks, and he knew it.

The troop was soon joined by two mounted police officers to escort them to their destination. Their horses, Echo and Eclipse, were friends of Sefton's. He tossed his head in greeting as they came into view. He took a deep breath of fresh morning air, his nostrils flaring. It was great to be alive and doing the job he was trained for. A job he loved.

Sefton didn't know that that morning he and his friends were destined never to reach Hyde Park Corner. A cruel and terrible event was about to happen that would change their lives for ever.

It took one minute to shatter Sefton's world for at ten forty exactly a nail-bomb, hidden by the Irish Republican Army inside a parked car and detonated by remote control, exploded as the soldiers and their horses passed by. All Sefton was aware of was a loud bang, a fireball flash, then nothing but pain and terror and confusion.

When the smoke cleared it became obvious that four Guardsmen and seven horses had been tragically killed. Echo and Eclipse and another horse called Copenhagen were badly injured. And Sefton? In the face of the blast, he somehow managed to stay on his feet, rocking slightly and dazed with pain and shock. The bodies of his companions lay all around him. Injured and bleeding men were wandering among them, others were lying on the ground, not moving. There was no sound. Only a horrific and deathly silence. Amazingly, Trooper Pedersen was still in the saddle, shocked and hardly able to move. He managed to get down and even though he had a nail through his hand, he held on to Sefton until help came. The horse had six inch nails embedded in his side, one in his head, chunks of metal in his neck. His eye was burned and a piece of razor sharp metal had sliced through a vein in his neck. He was bleeding to death. His once spotless white socks were covered in blood.

The brave horse didn't make a sound. He just stood there, head hanging down, until help arrived.

Weak and shattered, Sefton at last managed to walk slowly to a waiting horse box to be ferried painfully and slowly back to the safety of his stable. A vet rushed to give him first aid, to staunch the wound in his neck but the signs weren't good. The brave Sefton was given only a fifty/fifty chance of survival.

When people heard what had happened, Sefton became, for them, a symbol of hope and courage in the midst of all the horror. He was determined to live. He would not be destroyed by a terrorist bomb as so many of his friends and fellow horses had been. Even though he was walking in the valley of the shadow of death, he was determined to survive. In the peaceful quietness of his box and with the constant loving vigil of his carers, Sefton slowly began to recover. Even though he had the best attention possible, everyone knew that if it hadn't been for his own strong courage and determination, his wounds would not have healed.

During that time, he became a hero. The barracks received thousands of gifts. Flowers, cards, fruit and vegetables, a quarter of a million packets of peppermints. Sefton became a household name. He was in the papers, on TV and radio. There was so much stuff that a special room had to be set up and two officers were commandeered to see the press and receive the presents and cards. Money came in from all over the place, get well cards piled up like a snowdrift. Sefton's were pinned all over the door and walls of his box.

A couple of weeks later, Sefton and the other injured horses were fit enough to be taken to the countryside. There, Sefton gradually got back his health and his strength. And with his recovery, people too began to get over the shock and horror

of what had happened. But with the recovery of the nation's spirit, Sefton was not forgotten. His greatest moment came when he was invited to appear at the Horse of the Year show. Everyone's hearts turned over as he was led in under a blazing spotlight. His body and face still bore the scars of that dreadful day but in spite of that the horse looked magnificent. His coal black coat shone, his eyes were bright. His ears were alert and his nostrils flared as he caught the scent of the crowd's admiration. To the delight of the audience he gave a buck and a whinny for the sheer joy of being alive as the applause and cheers echoed round the arena. His character and spirit had been an inspiration to millions.

Every morning, since that terrible summer day, the soldiers of the Queen's Life Guard ride past the spot where the outrage took place. Now, they hold up their swords in memory and tribute to their comrades and horses that died so that they will never be forgotten.

Soon after Sefton's appearance at the Show, he joined them on duty again. Horses have long memories and it is another tribute to his spirit and courage that he passed that spot fearlessly and without batting an eyelid. He put his trust and his faith in his rider and the people who had worked together for his survival. And they, in

turn, put their trust in the worthy animal who
had become known as Sefton, the miracle horse.

BUCEPHALUS
the Conqueror's Horse

Alexander the Great is one of the most famous conquerors in ancient history. He was born in 356 BC in Greece. Almost as well-known as Alexander himself is his magnificent battle charger, Bucephalus. The story of the love between the king and Bucephalus is one of the most celebrated examples of the bond that can exist between a man and his heroic horse.

Alexander was the son of King Philip of Macedonia, a kingdom in northern Greece. Alexander loved horses and was always excited when the time came for the huge annual horse fair that was held in the ancient town of Pella where Alexander lived with his father in the royal palace. Horse traders and dealers from all over the known world came to this fair. It was there that the young Alexander first set eyes on the magnificent, coal black stallion he was later to name Bucephalus, a word that meant 'Ox head' because of the ox head shaped white blaze on the animal's forehead.

At that time, the horse was called Thunder and he caught Alexander's eye as soon as he was brought to the fair. He was the most magnificent animal the young prince had ever seen. High spirited, still almost wild, the horse tossed his black mane and tail and rolled his huge eyes in fear and bewilderment at the noise and crowds that surrounded him. Alexander watched in horror as the handlers shouted at the animal and tried to beat him. The prince's heart went out to the terrified, angry creature. He had been around horses for all of his young life and he knew this was not the way to treat them.

Earlier in the day, cavalry officers and tribal chiefs had been bidding hotly for the horses on sale. Many of them had looked at Thunder but decided the stallion was too wild. They needed well-mannered, well-trained horses for their armies. The more spirited animals were best left alone.

The fair was something of a day out for the

townspeople and crowds thronged the area. The whole town had a carnival atmosphere. There was a rumour that King Philip himself was on the lookout for a new battle charger and the people were hoping to get a glance of their king. Word of this had spread rapidly through the horse dealers and traders and they were anxious to show off their best horses. They quarrelled and argued over who was to parade their animals first. Everyone knew King Philip would pay a handsome price for the right one.

When Philip and his son arrived, the king spent a long time looking over the animals presented to him but none caught his eye. He didn't see one single horse he thought was worthy of a ride. He had almost given up when he spotted Thunder and ordered him to be brought before him.

One of the dealers led the animal forward but it was obvious the horse was still wild. He reared and whinnied and tossed his noble head showing the whites of his eyes. The crowd stood back in alarm. Wild horses had been known to snap their tethers and cause injury to the spectators in their frenzied bid to escape.

It was obvious that Thunder's owner had done his best to break the animal's spirit but he had used cruel methods which had only confused and terrified the animal. A vicious, spiked bit had been thrust into Thunder's mouth. He had been whipped cruelly under his belly where the trader hoped the wounds wouldn't show. It was no wonder that he reared and snorted to try to get away from his cold-blooded captors.

In spite of all this, Thunder was exactly the kind of horse the king had been looking for. Deep hooves, strong legs, a broad chest, a proud, arched neck and silky mane and tail that would shine like jet with good grooming. The horse wore a showy bridle but no saddle.

Philip gazed at Thunder shrewdly. He was an excellent judge of horses and knew exactly what he wanted. There was no doubt about it, the animal was splendid. He summoned his head groom to put Thunder through his paces.

The groom came forward carrying a saddle. But the horse refused to let him put it on. He shied away and snorted. Philip ordered the man to ride bareback but every time he tried to mount the animal it threw him to the ground.

All the time this was going on, Alexander was watching. He could see the horse was petrified. He understood how the barbaric treatment had made him scared of people and noise and even of his own shadow. Alexander wasn't at all surprised he wouldn't let anyone get on him. He hated all human beings. Everyone he had come

into contact with had caused him suffering. Alexander could see the animal quivering with rage and fear. Was this man going to beat him too?

After several attempts, the groom, bruised and shaken, gave up. Philip turned away in disgust, angry that a dealer should try to sell such a wild animal, let alone to a king! He called for his son and began to make his way back to the palace.

But the young prince had other ideas. He was furious at what he had seen and his heart was full of sorrow to see how the men had treated such a noble creature. The animal was being ruined. Alexander could see through his wildness and his rage. He wanted desperately to be given the chance to tame the stallion in a way he was sure would work. Kindness. It wasn't that he needed a horse – he was the prince and could have had any mount from the stables he wanted. He simply felt sorry for Thunder and wanted to show everyone what a little kindness and understanding could do.

As Philip began to leave, Alexander ran towards him. He begged his father to allow him to try to ride the big, black horse. Philip stared at him. He was only a boy. What could he do that the head groom couldn't? The servants chuckled to themselves. They thought it would be a grand joke to let the young prince try to ride the mad creature. If the horse threw him off it might take the boy down a peg or two. Philip heard them muttering amongst themselves. He knew Alexander was as brave as any boy of his age could be but he doubted even his own son would get anywhere with the crazed animal.

But Alexander was the son of a king and he had to set an example.

'Very well, Alexander,' Philip said. 'If you can ride him, I'll buy him for you. If not . . . well you can have him anyway but you must pay for him yourself.'

Alexander wasn't put off by his father's deal. He knew the trader wanted a very high price for Thunder but he was so confident that he could ride him he shook hands with his father to seal the bargain.

When the trader heard the deal being struck he was suddenly scared. Supposing the young prince was killed? The king might have him executed. He stepped forward to try to help but Alexander ordered him away. He knew the sight and scent of the man frightened the horse out of his wits. When the animal heard the name Thunder, he knew he was going to be hurt. The further away the dealer was, the better.

It was at that moment, even before he rode the

horse, that Alexander decided to change the animal's name. He would call him Bucephalus. He thought the name suited the horse well – he was as strong and as stubborn as an ox.

By now, people had heard what was going on and had flocked to the place where Alexander and Bucephalus stood face to face. Alexander told them to stay back then he moved forward softly to take hold of the reins. He whispered the horse's new name. Bucephalus. It had a gentle ring to it. A kind of whispering sound like the noise of the wind across the Grecian plains where the animal used to run wild. The horse's nostrils flared as he tried to catch the scent of the young human in front of him. He knew his hated master had gone away and already he seemed calmer.

The crowd held their breath as Alexander gently eased the pressure on the cruel bit. Then he slowly led the horse round to face the sun. He knew that as soon as Bucephalus could not be spooked by his own shadow he would stand still, still enough to allow Alexander to leap on his back and ride him away.

You could have heard a pin drop. Those men who had devoted all their lives to horses waited breathlessly for the boy prince to either be thrown off or run away with – they reckoned his only hope was to try to stay on while the horse galloped until it was exhausted. But neither of these things happened. Alexander was still speaking softly to the animal. It stood, ears pricked, blowing through its nostrils, watching every move the boy made. Then, to everyone's amazement, the animal lowered its head towards Alexander as he checked that the bridle wasn't too tight. Then, with one leap the boy was on his back. Amazingly, the horse stayed completely calm until the prince gave him a signal then he tossed his head and raced away to the east, hooves thundering on the dry ground until, in a cloud of dust, boy and animal disappeared out of sight.

The king couldn't believe his eyes. Where grown men had failed with cruelty, his son had succeeded with kindness. He waited proudly for Alexander and Bucephalus to return.

It was over an hour before they came back. After a short while, Philip had begun to get worried and had sent his fastest riders after them. But they had returned, unable to catch up with Alexander and Bucephalus.

At last, horse and rider were spotted heading back to town. A great cheer went up from the crowd as they came into view. Bucephalus was sweating but relaxed and completely under control. He held his head proudly as his new young master dismounted cavalry style by swinging one leg over the animal's neck. He stood in front of the king grinning triumphantly. Alexander the Great had made his first conquest.

Philip gave the dealer his asking price and Bucephalus became Alexander's horse for the rest of the animal's life.

After that, Alexander and Bucephalus never spent a day apart. Alexander never forgot the lesson the animal had taught him. That you can achieve more by kindness than by cruelty. He had ridden a horse that had seemed impossible to ride and it is said that this inspired him in his many campaigns.

When Alexander was nineteen years old, his father was murdered by his enemies from Asia and he became king of Macedonia. It was on Bucephalus that he set out with a great army of horsemen to seek revenge for his father's death. Bucephalus carried him from Greece to Persia, then on to Egypt where he founded the great sea port of Alexandria and married the Pharoah's daughter. Then he and his armies made their way across Afghanistan and on to the great continent of India.

Bucephalus carried Alexander faithfully for many thousands of kilometres. He would never allow anyone else to ride him and the bond between king and horse grew as the years went by. When Bucephalus finally died, Alexander honoured him by naming a city after him. The city was called Bucephala and it served as a lasting memorial to the courage of the great war horse that helped his master to conquer the world.

GOLDFLAKE

the mare who had sparks in her hooves

Arthur Elliot had always loved horses. He lived on a small farm in Cornwall and had owned and trained them for many years. He also taught people to ride and every year he organised a gymkhana for the local children. In fact Arthur was never far from his beloved animals and was known locally as the 'Hoss' man.

One day, Arthur told his mum he had one ambition. That was to ride the length of Britain, from Land's End which was close to his home in Carbis Bay, to John o'Groats in Scotland. It would be a journey of over six hundred kilometres. And Arthur knew there was only one horse he could trust to take him on this journey – his eight-year-old chestnut mare, Goldflake. Goldflake was fit and strong and devoted to him. She was always eager to please and Arthur knew she would not let him down.

When Arthur told his mother what he wanted to do she thought it was a great idea. Arthur thought people had forgotten how strong and trusty a horse could be and it was for this reason he wanted to do the journey. At that time lots of people had decided to travel from one end of the country to the other but they had done it in cars and on bikes, even on foot. But no-one so far had done it on a horse.

'There were times,' Arthur said to his mother, 'when people had to rely on horses to take them everywhere. If I do this ride it'll remind people how horses can still do their stuff.'

Even though it was only forty years ago, Britain was a very different place in which to live. Not many people owned their own cars although they were becoming more common. There weren't any motorways and people mostly travelled by train or coach. Very few people owned a TV and those who did had to watch programmes in black and white. People learned about the world from the radio and newspapers.

Although Arthur's mum thought his ride was a good idea, when he told his friends what he proposed to do they thought he was joking. They scoffed at him and told him the mare would never make it. They even put bets on with one another. Several of them offered to lend him a bigger, stronger horse than Goldflake but Arthur wouldn't hear of it. He knew his mare could do it. She was a very special 'one-man' horse and she wouldn't let him down. His friends were still scornful and none of them believed the event would take place.

But Arthur had made up his mind and he began to make plans for the journey. He would show his friends that they were wrong!

And so, on Saturday, August 21st, 1955, Arthur and Goldflake set out on their historic ride. That particular week, Cornwall was in the grip of a heatwave although it hadn't been especially sunny up until then. As a result, St Ives was packed with holidaymakers. On the Tuesday before, three thousand people had turned up to watch water sports held in St Ives harbour to celebrate the diamond anniversary of the Town Band.

By now, the local newspaper, the St Ives Times, had got hold of Arthur's story and residents and visitors alike lined the streets to wave as Arthur and Goldflake trotted by. Sparks flew from the mare's hooves as she passed, eager to be on her way to the adventure her master had planned. As they disappeared down the road, Arthur's friends shook their heads in doubt and dismay. They were convinced he would never make it to Scotland.

But they were wrong and during the long journey that lay ahead Arthur's faith in his horse was well rewarded even though the trek proved to be far more difficult than he had imagined.

Arthur hoped to do the journey in about six weeks. He planned to ride about twenty kilometres a day, stopping at farms and inns on the way where he would do some work in return for food and lodging for himself and his horse. The news of his record attempt had spread and there had been reports in newspapers all over the country. As horse and rider passed through villages and towns, people came out to cheer them on their way. Arthur sometimes felt like royalty as they craned their necks eagerly to see Goldflake pass by. She always seemed to know she was the centre of attention and trotted along smartly, the sparks flying from her hooves as she clip-clopped past. She seemed proud to be making history and delighted to be spending so much time with her master.

Everywhere Arthur and Goldflake went, they made friends. People were happy to provide food and shelter and begged Arthur to call in on his return journey. Goldflake was petted and fussed and admired for her stamina on this long ride. She loved every minute of it even though she did get tired out at times.

Then, six weeks after they set off, they had their first setback.

When they arrived at the place where they had planned to spend the night, to Arthur's dismay he found the mare had a very sore back where the saddle had been rubbing her skin. He knew they would have to stop there for a while to let the wound heal. It would mean that the journey would take longer than planned but his horse's health was the most important thing. Luckily, he had friends in the area where he could stay until Goldflake was better. Arthur wrote to a friend back in Cornwall telling him he hoped to begin the ride again before long.

By the time they set off again, the summer was over and the weather had turned into the grey, chilly days of Autumn. In spite of this, Arthur was full of enthusiasm. It was great to be out on the road again. He wrote to his friend that the best way to see the countryside was from the back of a horse. He enjoyed riding along the country lanes and seeing the different types of farms along the way.

After his delay, Arthur was anxious to get on. He knew winter was on its way and it could be very bleak and bitterly cold in Scotland at that time of the year. If they didn't make better progress they might not be back in Cornwall for Christmas. And he didn't want his scornful friends to think they weren't going to make it. He was absolutely determined to prove them wrong.

Sadly though, something else happened to hold them up. They hadn't even reached the next county when Goldflake was frightened by a dog jumping over a hedge. She reared up in terror, tipping Arthur out of the saddle and landing heavily back down on her front legs. Arthur dislocated his shoulder and Goldflake injured herself in the fall. By the time they were both well enough to carry on, the days were getting shorter and in Scotland, the winter was threatening to arrive early. For a while it looked as if Arthur and Goldflake might be gone a lot longer than anyone thought.

But things got better for a while and soon they were crossing the boundary of the old city of York where Arthur and his mare were greeted with enthusiasm. Their fame had spread as far as the border counties and they were warmly welcomed at farms and inns along the northern route. Arthur wore a sash saying 'Lands End to John o'Groats' so there was no mistaking the lone horse and rider coming along the street. Everyone was anxious to hear tales of their exploits and to provide a warm stable for Goldflake and a room for Arthur. In return Arthur would entertain them with a few Cornish songs and folk tales.

By the time they reached the Scottish borders an early winter had set in. Blizzards forced them to stop and even when they did manage to get going again, things were really difficult. Arthur began to realise why his friends had doubted him. By now, the mare was weary and plodding through the deep snow exhausted her. But Arthur urged her gently on. They only had a few lonely kilometres to go before they reached John o'Groats and he knew she could make it.

For the last few hours of their journey, Arthur and Goldflake didn't see another living soul. The landscape was bare and bleak and bitterly cold. The snow had given way to sharp needles of rain and the going was muddy and slippery. Arthur was never so pleased in all his life when a building suddenly loomed out of the mist and the John o'Groats hotel came into view. He felt a surge of happiness. They were there – his faithful mare hadn't let him down.

The first thing Arthur did when Goldflake plodded wearily into the courtyard was to jump down and give her a hug. 'Well done, lass!' he exclaimed triumphantly. 'We've done it at last.' Arthur and his horse had been on the road for over two months.

'I'm the proudest man in Britain,' Arthur declared to the onlookers as he unsaddled the mare and led her into the warmth and comfort of her stable. After he had rubbed her down and fed her he spent the evening telling the hotel people about his adventures. They were full of admiration and when Arthur phoned his friends at home to tell them the good news they could hardly believe their ears. They had been wrong after all. Arthur and his faithful horse were heroes!

When they had rested, Arthur began making

plans for their journey back. He knew it would be too much for Goldflake to go all the way home on foot so he made arrangements for her to be transported back by train. She would be unloaded at a station just outside St Ives and he would ride her the last kilometre or two triumphantly into the town.

Back in St Ives, plans were underway to welcome the heroic Arthur and Goldflake home. The streets were decked with flags and balloons and the people waited excitedly to see them. Arthur was their local hero and they were determined to let him know how proud they were of him and his faithful mare, Goldflake.

But there was to be another hiccup in Arthur's plans. The weather again intervened.

On the day the mare was due to arrive at the station the weather was grim. A thick fog covered the landscape and the train was late arriving at the station. Everything was ready. People lined the streets and the mayor of St Ives, decked out in his chain of office, was waiting at a place called Trelyon to greet them. He began to get impatient. He had a meeting that afternoon and couldn't wait for ever. Finally he gave up and left.

But the townsfolk remained and when the train eventually arrived their patience was rewarded. During the delay, Arthur had gone to have a drink at the local inn and when he heard the train's whistle he suddenly realised just how late it was. He hurriedly unloaded Goldflake and saddled her up. He mounted quickly and urged her into a trot, then a canter. The waiting crowds began to cheer as they heard the clatter of horse's hooves coming along the street. Then Goldflake came into view, sparks flying from her hooves as she cantered into town. The hero and his horse were home!

Later on, Arthur and Goldflake finally got to meet the mayor when they visited him at his place of work. He congratulated them on their magnificent ride. Arthur gave Goldflake another big hug. He knew that no other horse would have carried him so faithfully, so far and that the story of Goldflake and her historic trek would go down in the history of Cornish tales.

And as for Arthur's scornful friends? They were as pleased as anyone to see him back home and didn't mind losing their bets one little bit.

CHARLEY
the horse who was wild at heart

When American artist, traveller and pioneer, George Catlin, first set eyes on a showy and prancing cream coloured mustang he knew he had to buy him. George was fascinated by Native Americans and had made drawing and recording their culture his life's work. It was the first quarter of the nineteenth century and the 'wild west' of America was just beginning to open up. The beautiful horse was just the animal George needed to carry him on his expeditions across the prairies to meet and record the native tribes. The wild looking mustang fitted the bill perfectly.

George soon discovered that the horse belonged to an army colonel who was only too pleased to sell the animal. The colonel had found him far too spirited and too wild to handle. The horse was a Comanche mustang called Charley and had been taken from the wild by the Comanche tribe. The Comanches were the greatest horsemen of all the Native Americans. George and the colonel agreed a price and the horse was his. In one of his famous illustrated books, George described the horse as 'showy' and that's exactly what he was. His pale coat gleamed in the sunshine, his black mane and tail were long and flowing. He held his head proudly as if he was still a member of a wild herd. George felt it was an honour to ride such a horse. Heads turned wherever they went.

George and Charley became a well-known pair on their many expeditions into previously un-explored territories. George never rode another horse and his faith in his Comanche mount was rewarded when he took Charley on a long trek to visit the Wichita tribe that lived on the edge of the Rocky Mountains where water and grass were scarce. He went there with a US Army expedition and while the soldiers' horses were drooping and looking sorry for themselves, Charley pranced along as bright as ever. George knew no other horse would have withstood the rigours of such a long trek so well. Once again, he thanked his lucky stars he had been able to buy Charley. He knew there was a bond between him and his horse that was something really special.

In 1834, George and Charley went with an army expedition to contact and make friends with more Native American tribes. George was full of excitement as the men and wagons set off from Fort Gibson on the Arkansas river. Charley felt George's excitement and pranced along at the head of the long string of horsemen. They had all their goods with them. Food and water, gifts for the tribes they came across. Most precious of all to George was his sketchbook safely tucked away in his saddle bag. Without it he wouldn't be able to record the lives of the Native Peoples and do the job he'd set out to do.

The long expedition was a great success. Charley loved every minute of it. The long treks through the grassy plains must have reminded him of the days when he was wild and free. His mane and tail flowed in the wind, his nostrils quivered with the scent of fresh air.

But as it turned out, there was a high price to pay. Over a third of the soldiers died after drinking contaminated water. Many of the horses died too. It was a sad line of sick men and horses that eventually struggled their way back to Fort Gibson. Among them was George, stricken by fever but managing to stay in the saddle. Luckily, Charley had escaped the sickness.

Their problems didn't end there. The sickness continued to rage through men and horses, causing dizziness and high fever. More died. George survived but wasn't getting any better. After a few weeks he decided only one thing would cure him. A journey home to Alton, Mississippi, over eight hundred kilometres away. And he knew only one horse could take him there. Charley.

George ordered his mustang to be fetched from his paddock where he had been grazing since the return to Fort Gibson. George packed the saddle bags. Coffee, ham and biscuits. There would be plenty of fodder for Charley . . . the prairie grass, fresh water from the streams and rivers they would have to cross. Still weak from his illness, George mounted Charley and they set off.

It was a grand early autumn day as man and horse left the fort on their epic journey. The soldiers watched them go, shaking their heads in disbelief. The man was mad. He would never make it. But they were wrong. Everyone but George had underestimated Charley. Eight hundred kilometres was a mere step to a fine, showy, Comanche horse like him!

George's many expeditions had taught him lots of things. He was a good trapper; he had his gun

and fishing rod. He knew he could live off the
land. In his bag he had a compass and was sure
he would find the way. He carried a bear skin rug
and a buffalo blanket to keep himself warm. His
saddle would be a makeshift pillow and Charley
was to be his friend and companion. What more
could a man want? He felt confident as he turned
Charley northwards into the endless sea of waving
grass. Every step would take him closer to home.
If his fever returned he would just make camp
and wait until he felt better again before resuming
his journey.

George and Charley were to travel for twenty

five days without seeing another human being.

George would often stop to sketch a landscape that took his eye while Charley would graze peacefully close by. The horse never seemed to tire. They had no problems with food. Plenty of grass, plenty of fresh water to drink and boil up for a mug of coffee on a fire of driftwood George would find along the river banks. He would unsaddle Charley and tie him to a stake on a long rein so the horse could graze to his heart's content. Before settling down to sleep, he would bring Charley close. If there was any emergency, the horse would be on hand. Quite often they would hear the eerie howling of wolves and George would bank up the fire to keep it going all night long. But it was late summer and food for wolves was plentiful too. Man and horse were never attacked although the wolves would often scavenge their camp once they had left.

From time to time, George's fever would come back and he would have to tether Charley and wait until his shaking and chattering had passed. But the attacks grew less and less frequent. The fresh air, the landscape of green grass and Charley's companionship were having a healing effect. George knew that by the time he reached home, he would be completely well. He had grown so attached to the big Comanche horse that he felt Charley knew what he was thinking. Often he would do something ... stop or turn, before George had asked him to. During those twenty five long days George thought he had learned all there was to know about the horse's character. He was loyal, intelligent, strong and well behaved. What George didn't take into account though, was that Charley had a will of his own. He was to learn the hard way.

He had just set up camp one night when Charley decided to show a side of his character that George hadn't encountered before. The mustang had always been spirited and energetic, his wild origins only just hidden beneath the surface. That was why George loved him so much. But this particular night the horse took it into his head to slip out of his head collar and run away. George didn't really know why he'd decided to do it. Maybe it was a case of the grass being greener on the other side of the fence. But out there on the wild prairie there were no fences, only acres and acres of open grassland. But whatever it was, that night Charley wanted to choose his own grazing area. And that area was a long way from the camp. Everyone who has ever tried to catch an independent horse knows how annoying it can be to get just within catching distance only to have the animal gallop off out of reach. 'Not likely,' Charley seemed to say as George got close to him time and time again. 'I'm grazing where I want to, tonight!'

Eventually George gave up. He settled down for the night by the fire with a heavy heart. He needed Charley but Charley needed him too. If there were any hungry wolves out there, the horse would be too far away for the man to protect him. George convinced himself that in the morning Charley would be gone. He would never see him again. What on earth had he done to upset his faithful companion? He gave a sigh and drifted off to sleep. There was no getting away from it. He would have to do the rest of the journey on foot.

It was in the middle of the night when George awoke with a start. A dark shadow loomed over him. Then he realised it was Charley. The horse was staring at him as if to make sure he was all right. He didn't know whether the horse was feeling guilty at playing him up or feeling suddenly scared to be out on the prairie all alone. George stretched out his hand but Charley galloped off again. George sighed. The lure of freedom had been too much for Charley. After all, he had once been a wild horse, galloping freely across the plains. Maybe it was this memory that made him wary of losing his freedom again.

The horse was still wild at heart.

But in the morning, Charley was still there, grazing in the distance. George decided there was only one thing for it. He would call Charley's bluff. He made a great show of packing up the camp. Banging saucepans together, putting his things into the bags. He picked up his gun, slung the heavy saddle across his back and set off on foot. George recounts what happened next in one of his books.

'Charley was standing with head and tail very high, looking at me and at the spot where the camp fire still burned. . . . He at length walked with a hurried step to the spot and seeing everything had gone began to neigh very violently and at last started off at the fullest speed and overtook me, passing within a few paces of me and wheeling about in front of me, trembling like an aspen leaf.'

George's heart was pounding as he called Charley's name and went slowly forward. Then he heaved a sigh of relief as the horse let him put on the saddle and bridle. He didn't scold him. He understood his need for independence.

From then on there was no more trouble. They camped that night in a beautiful valley. George found some old stones that told him it had once been a Native burial ground. But he wasn't scared of ghosts and settled down to sleep with Charley close by. They were on the last leg of their epic journey and would soon be heading for home.

The next stop was a tiny settlement called Kickapoo where Charley was to show George yet another side of his character. This time he was to show courage that took away George's breath.

At Kickapoo, the landscape was different. There were many streams and fast flowing rivers to cross. They had to go through marshy, waterlogged ground where they couldn't tell whether the water was one metre or ten metres deep. Charley didn't put a foot wrong and plunged bravely forward. George relied on his horse's wild instincts to guide him safely across this land full of danger. Once, after heavy rain, they had to cross the Osage River. The river had become a raging torrent. George unsaddled his horse and pushed him forward. He plunged in without hesitation, understanding he was meant to swim to the other side. Maybe he remembered again the time when he was part of a wild herd, crossing dangerous waters to safe grazing on the far distant shore. To George's horror, the current took Charley a kilometre downstream and out of sight. Once again, he thought he would never see his beloved horse again.

George hurriedly roped together some wood

to hold on to while he crossed the river with the saddle and bags. He scrambled up the far bank, his eyes searching desperately for signs of Charley. He shouted with joy when he spotted him waiting patiently for his master to arrive. He was none the worse for his dangerous swim.

It wasn't long before there was another torrent to cross. This time George decided to swim with Charley. The water was so wide and so deep the horse's hooves didn't touch the bottom once. Worse still, when they reached the other side the bank was too steep for Charley to climb. Fearing again for his horse's life, George hung on to the reins while Charley swam downstream until he found a place where he could clamber out. Once again his determination and bravery had triumphed. After a hug and a good rub down, he was none the worse for his adventure.

At last George and Charley reached the end of their long journey. They arrived at Boonville, Missouri, crossed to New Franklin, then travelled on easier ground to Alton on the Mississippi river where George's wife was waiting. She was amazed to see George looking so well and even more amazed when she heard how bravely Charley had carried her husband the eight hundred kilometre trek home.

George Catlin never forgot that journey and

his courageous Comanche horse, Charley. He counted it as one of the best things that ever happened to him in all of his life. He knew that the animal's courage and loyalty came from that wildness that no man could ever really tame and he always thought of Charley as the mustang who was wild at heart.

PHAR LAP

the horse who gave people hope

Seventy years ago, on a lovely spring day in October in Timaru, New Zealand, a brood mare called Entreaty went into labour. The vet was called and soon the mare gave birth to a beautiful, long-legged chestnut foal. Entreaty's owner was delighted. He was a racehorse breeder and the foal, a colt, had all the makings of a champion. He looked strong and had an intelligent expression in his eyes.

The new colt was soon up and about, wobbling around the stable on his gangly legs. And when Entreaty had recovered from the birth and the two animals were led outside, their owner was even more pleased. Even though the young one was hardly more than a few hours old he was full of energy and spirit. The man knew he would fetch a good price.

Two years later, the foal, who had been named Phar Lap, was entered into the local bloodstock auction. Racehorse owners and trainers came from all over New Zealand and Australia to be at the sale. Among them was a man called Hugh Telford. He was there on behalf of his brother, Harry, a racehorse trainer who lived in Sydney, Australia. Harry hadn't been able to get to the sale and had asked Hugh to look out for any young horses that might one day turn out to be a champion.

As soon as Hugh spotted the young chestnut he knew he should bid for him. There was something about him, the long legs, his obvious intelligence, that gave Hugh shivers down his spine. Phar Lap was a bit skinny and wild and obviously needed a lot of training but Hugh could see beyond this. He knew the horse could one day be a champion.

Hugh was a fine judge of horses but even he couldn't possibly have known just how good a winner this young horse would turn out to be.

When the bidding began Hugh was surprised that no-one else seemed interested in the colt. And when he was able to buy him for a hundred and seventy pounds he was delighted. Even though, in those days, this was quite a lot of money, he knew he'd got a bargain. When he told his brother Harry the news, Harry decided he would sell the colt on to another Australian trainer, David Davies. Racehorse owners often sold animals on when they hadn't got enough time to train the horses themselves. Harry managed to persuade David that his brother was convinced the horse could one day be a champion.

And so, without even seeing him, David became the owner of the chestnut colt, Phar Lap. The horse was put on board a steamship and taken to Australia.

By the time he reached Sydney, Phar Lap looked a mess. The voyage had been rough and conditions on the ship were poor. When David first saw the horse, he was horrified. Phar Lap seemed a clumsy bundle of skin and bone and he had warts all over his face from a virus he had picked up on the ship. He had loved the fresh air and open spaces of New Zealand and hated being cooped up below deck. He had been too frightened to eat and his legs were stiff from lack of exercise.

When David saw the horse, he was furious. He had been a fool to let Harry Telford persuade him into buying such a poor looking animal.

It had been a waste of money.

When Harry heard how angry David was he felt guilty. It was really his brother's fault. He had bought the colt in the first place and Harry had trusted his judgement.

So Harry struck a deal with David. The two men agreed that Harry should lease Phar Lap from him for three years. Harry would pay for all the animal's training, while David would get a third of all the prize money the horse won. Harry knew Phar Lap had got a good pedigree and was still convinced it would be worth spending time and money training him.

Neither man knew it but Phar Lap was going to make them very rich indeed.

When the chestnut arrived at Harry's stables he was met by a young stable boy, Tom Woodcock. When Tom saw him being unloaded in the stable yard, he had a strange feeling. Beyond that bony exterior was a horse with a big heart. Tom had been around horses long enough to know that. He went up to him and stroked him. As Phar Lap snickered into his hand Tom felt there was a bond between them. He was elated when his boss, Harry, said he could be Phar Lap's special groom. As he led the horse into its new stable he felt a pang of excitement. Looking after this horse was going to be great!

But things didn't go too well at first. Phar Lap, or 'Bobby' as Tom had nicknamed him, turned out to be a pain in the neck. He was docile and lazy and showed no inclination to trot, let alone gallop. He played tricks on Tom, whipping off his cap with his teeth when the boy wasn't looking, knocking over his water bucket on purpose. But none of that made any difference. Tom knew 'Bobby' was a special horse – all he needed was time. And as time went by that special bond grew until they were so close to one another that 'Bobby' refused to eat his food unless Tom was in the stable with him. Tom was happy that he and the young horse had become such good friends. Even though he was only a stable boy Tom thought of Phar Lap as his own special horse. That bond between them was to last all of Phar Lap's life.

Once he had settled down, Phar Lap began to show signs of the champion he would become. Weeks of training and good food had improved him no end. By now he was fully grown. He was seventeen hands high and had powerful leg muscles and a strong heart. Out on gallops with other racehorses he always wanted to be the one in front. This was a sure sign of a champion.

By the end of February, 1929, he was ready for his first race.

The word 'Phar Lap' means 'wink of the skies',

or 'lightning' in the Thai language and even though the horse wasn't placed in his first few races, when he ran at a place called Rosehill, in April of that same year, he lived up to his name. He came first. It looked as if Harry's hunch had been right.

Two years later, when Phar Lap had already won many races and his fame had spread far and wide, there was a great depression in the economy of Australia and New Zealand and many other countries in the world. Hundreds of farms and companies were going out of business. Industries went bankrupt and by 1932 one quarter of the whole of Australia's population had no jobs and no money. Many families couldn't pay their rent and had to leave their homes to find shelter where they could. The roads were full of people with trailers loaded with their worldly goods setting off to try to find work for themselves and their families in other parts of the country. Unlike today there was no welfare state to provide money for these people. Handouts were mainly of food and they were often only given to men who worked on special government projects such as building roads or railways. They hated receiving charity and felt humiliated to be given food instead of wages. Things were very grim indeed.

For many of these, there was one light in their

darkness. If they could scrape enough money together to bet on Phar Lap winning a race, then they might win enough money to feed their families and maybe find a place to live. He was a symbol of hope and good luck to these desperate people. He had won most of the most famous races in Australia and had stood as the favourite in all of them. They simply couldn't lose!

Although Phar Lap was helping people through their bad times, he wasn't popular with everyone. Because so many people were winning money, it meant that the bookmakers lost a fortune and on Derby Day, 1930, someone tried to kill him. Tom knew it was a day he would never forget.

Tom was bringing Phar Lap back from a practice gallop when a car roared along the road and pulled up beside them. Tom was riding a pony and had Phar Lap beside him on a lead rein. Tom knew at once something was wrong and that his beloved horse was in danger. As he pulled the pony across to try to protect Phar Lap, shots were fired from the car's open window. As the pony panicked, Tom was thrown off but he managed to hang on to Phar Lap as the car sped away. Luckily, neither of the horses, nor Tom, was hurt and no-one ever discovered who had tried to kill them. People thought it was someone hired by the bookmakers but this could never be proved.

Tom knew they had all had a very narrow escape.

It was soon after this that Harry decided to take Phar Lap to America to try his luck there. Because he knew the horse would never be happy without Tom, he told him he was to go with him. In the stable, Tom gave the champion a hug. He knew he wouldn't have been able to bear it if they had to be separated. And he knew Phar Lap wouldn't be happy with anyone else looking after him.

The people of Australia were sad to see their hero leave. Everyone hoped that one day he would come back to run again in his home country. Sadly, this was not to be.

By now, the horse was so famous and successful

that he was given VIP treatment during his voyage to America and arrived fit and healthy. His first race was in March, 1932, when thousands turned out to watch him win the Agua Calienti cup in New Mexico. As they cheered him past the winning post no-one had any idea that his would be his very last race.

After his success, the champion was taken to California to rest. His owner felt he deserved it. Phar Lap had won thirty seven of his fifty one races in four years and badly needed a break. David was making plans for him to take part in other races and for a series of films to be made about his famous horse.

One morning Tom went to Phar Lap's stable to feed him and found him looking ill. He had a feeling of dread. The horse was pacing around in his stable and was obviously in great pain. He hurriedly called the vet but by the time he arrived, the champion had died. Tom was heartbroken. How could this terrible thing happen to his beloved horse?

Although it was never proved, it was thought that Phar Lap had been poisoned by a jealous racehorse owner. There were other theories too. One was that his grass had been contaminated by someone spraying weedkiller nearby. But no-one ever knew for sure why Phar Lap had died.

When the people of Australia heard the terrible news they were stunned. Phar Lap had been a ray of hope during their dark times and they found it hard to come to terms with such a great tragedy. They wanted him brought home and so the great champion's last journey began.

Today, Phar Lap is remembered with pride by the Australian people. He had the character and strength of a true sporting hero. If you were to visit the museum of Victoria you would see him there today. His hide was mounted and he has a section of the museum all to himself. He has drawn millions of people to the museum from all over the world. The visitors include Tom Woodcock himself who donated his own souvenirs of his beloved horse to the museum. Several films and many books have been written about Phar Lap and even today people all over the world think of him as Australia's greatest sporting hero ever.

WEEDIE
the brave donkey who saved her friend's life . . . twice

Weedie, a sweet-tempered grey donkey, was already quite old when she arrived at a donkey sanctuary a few years ago. She had been rescued and taken there in a sorry state after she had been abandoned by her owner and left to fend for herself. She was thin and weak and could hardly walk when she was discovered by the sanctuary's owners. But with good food and loving care the old jenny donkey soon became fit and healthy again and spent many hours running with the other donkeys at the farm.

One day another elderly donkey arrived. This one was a lot older than Weedie. Her name was

Grannie and she was pure white. No-one was sure exactly how old she was but it was obvious she was very elderly indeed. She was wobbly on her feet and her heart was no longer strong. Her eyesight was very bad and she wasn't able to digest normal donkey food and had to be kept on a special diet.

In spite of her ailments and poor eyesight the newcomer managed to run with Weedie and the other rescued donkeys in the meadows surrounding the farm. Donkeys are, by nature, herd animals and Grannie was happy to be with her friends. She managed very well.

Eventually, though, it became clear that Grannie had gone almost completely blind. She was observed bumping into fences and into other donkeys. They began to bully her and it was decided that she would be safer away from the rest of the herd. Grannie was put in a field nearer to the farmhouse so the owners could keep an eye on her. For company, Weedie was put in the field with her. The two old donkeys soon became firm friends. They could be seen grazing contentedly together in the pasture and the owners were happy that the two would live out the rest of their lives together in peace and happiness.

Soon after this, though, it became obvious that

Grannie could no longer distinguish between light and dark, or make out any movement around her. She had finally totally lost her sight. It was then that the friendship between the two donkeys became a matter of great importance. Weedie would literally be Grannie's eyes. If the older of the two donkeys became alone and confused on the far side of the meadow, she would only have to bray loudly and Weedie would go galloping to the rescue. If Grannie couldn't locate her special hay, Weedie would nudge her towards it so she didn't go hungry.

As the bond between the two old jenny donkeys grew stronger, the owners of the sanctuary saw that they could rely on Weedie to protect Grannie and they let them graze a bigger pasture away from the house. They felt sure that if Grannie encountered any problems, the younger jenny would soon let them know. One day, they were proved right.

It was late afternoon when one of the owners came back from a shopping trip. She was surprised to see Weedie by the fence, all alone. She sensed at once that something was wrong. The two donkeys were usually inseparable. Then Weedie began to bray loudly and urgently. She ran up and down the fence, shook her head and carried on braying. The owner hurriedly got into her jeep and drove across to the far end of the field with Weedie in hot pursuit. Sure enough, her hunch had been right. When she reached the far end she found Grannie had fallen into a ditch and couldn't get out. The owner tried to haul her out but couldn't manage it by herself. She quickly jumped back into her jeep and drove back to the farm to get help from a neighbour. In no time at all, the man was at Grannie's side with his tractor. With the aid of ropes and a winch, the old donkey was soon up on her feet again. She was shaken but unhurt. Weedie nuzzled her friend as if to say, there you are, don't worry, I'll always be there for you. Everyone knew that if it hadn't been for Weedie, Grannie would have died. The owners were amazed at Weedie's intelligence and courage. Little did they know that in a short while, Weedie would again save her old friend's life.

When Grannie had recovered from her ordeal the two animals were again allowed to graze outside although this time they were kept closer to the house. Although the owners knew they could rely on Weedie to protect her friend, they felt more at ease if they could keep an eye on both donkeys themselves.

One cold and windy spring day the owner was concerned that Grannie might catch a chill so she went to the tack room to fetch a blanket to put over her. She went through the gate and ran across the paddock to find Grannie, the blanket flapping in the wind. As the owner hurried towards the two donkeys Grannie suddenly lifted her head in fright. She had been startled by the sudden thud of footsteps and the strange noise of the flapping blanket. To the owner's horror, she galloped off, right towards the top of a steep slope which she normally wouldn't have gone near. The owner realised then that Grannie could still make out moving shadows and it had been the dancing shadow of the flapping blanket that had scared her away. The owner had a sudden, frightening vision of Grannie hurtling over the

top of the slope and toppling down the other side. She called and called but the old donkey was too far away to hear. As the owner ran after her, her heart thudded with fear. If Grannie was hurt it would be her fault. She would never forgive herself.

But she hadn't reckoned on Weedie. As she ran towards Grannie, Weedie galloped past her. The donkey reached the top of the slope and about three metres from the edge of the sharp drop on the other side she placed herself firmly in front of Grannie. The old, blind donkey could go no further. Weedie stood there, refusing to budge, until the owner caught up and gently led Grannie away. If it hadn't been for Weedie the older animal would have hurtled over the top and possibly been killed. As the two donkeys were led back to safety, the owner heaved a sigh of relief. A younger donkey might have survived such a fall but she knew that Grannie wouldn't have done. Weedie had saved her friend's life for a second time.

She was a real hero!

Back at the farm, the owner gave Weedie a big hug and stroked her long, adorable ears. She knew that behind that broad grey donkey chest beat a brave heart of purest gold.

MISTY
the wild pony who helped save a whole herd

On the salty, sea-swept Atlantic barrier island of Assateague just off the coast of Virginia in the USA lives a herd of wild ponies. The island, and its smaller, sister island Chincoteague, is separated from the mainland by a deep sea channel. People live on the smaller island but Assateague is a wildlife sanctuary and inhabited only by water fowl and the pony herd.

Some people say that the ponies that live on the island are descendants of horses that escaped from a shipwrecked Spanish galleon hundreds of years ago, others that they have descended from ponies let loose by the early settlers. But however they came to be there, the wild ponies of Assateague are well known all over the world because one in particular, a brown and white filly called Misty, had a famous children's book written about her. And because she was so well known, Misty was able to help raise money to buy new ponies when half the herd was lost in a terrible storm.

Misty's story begins at the end of one July when the wild ponies are rounded up by the local people and swum across the channel from Assateague to Chincoteague, a distance of about half a kilometre. This is part of a famous event called 'Pony Penning Day' when some of the ponies are taken from the herd to be sold. This is done every year as the island can only support about a hundred and fifty horses. Otherwise there wouldn't be enough natural food for them to eat. The ponies, once tamed, have very friendly natures and make good pets and riding ponies.

This round up is an exciting event in the area. People come from all over the country to see the Pony Swim, maybe buy a pony and have fun at the carnival and fair that takes place at the same time. The local volunteer fire department who own the pony herd organise the carnival to raise funds for new equipment and to pay veterinary surgeons to make sure the animals are in good health. Every year about fifty young ponies are sold and it was at the auction that children's writer, Marguerite Henry first saw Misty and fell in love with her.

At that time, Misty was very young and had been brought from her island across the causeway by truck with her mother, Phantom, as the foal was too small to swim by herself. She was only a few weeks old. Misty had big brown eyes, golden eyelashes and a bright gold patch round one eye. Mrs Henry thought she was enchanting. The author had planned to write a book about a wild pony and she knew at once that Misty was the one she wanted to feature in her story. As Mrs Henry watched the auction she learned that Phantom and Misty had been sold to a man who people called Grandpa Beebe and his two grandchildren. When the bidding was over she asked him if she could buy Misty and take her home to the small house and meadow in Illinois where she lived so she could study her as she was writing. Grandpa Beebe refused. Misty was too young to be taken from her mother. Mrs Henry was disappointed but she made a bargain with Misty's new owner . . . she would wait until Misty was a little older, then when Misty herself could have foals of her own, she would send her back to

Chincoteague. Grandpa Beebe agreed and the deal was struck.

And so Mrs Henry went home to Illinois to begin writing about the little foal she had fallen in love with. Every day she thought about Misty, back in Chincoteague with her mother, Phantom. Although she started the book she couldn't wait until Misty was grazing outside in the paddock so she could look out of her window and see her. She had already decided on a title for her story. It was to be called 'Misty of Chincoteague' and the highlight of the book was to be the exciting pony swim across the channel between the two islands. She had decided to use real people as characters. Grandpa Beebe and his grandchildren Paul and Maureen were all to be in the story. Some of the other people on Chincoteague were to be in it too. The volunteer firefighters and the fishermen who all became cowboys on the day of the exciting round up. Although Mrs Henry hoped the book would be a success, she had no idea then, just how much of a hit it would be.

When November came, Misty was at last old enough to leave Phantom and go to Illinois to be with Mrs Henry. It was then that the story really came to life. Mrs Henry could see the young pony outside her window now and the character of Misty just grew and grew.

A few weeks later, the book was finished. When it was published it was a success straight away. It seemed everyone wanted to read Misty's story and soon almost all the children in the country knew about her and the wild pony round up at Chincoteague. A film was made about them and Misty became a star. She went round visiting schools and libraries and even learned to do tricks to make the children laugh. She would put her legs up on a little stool and offer her hoof to 'shake hands' with people. Everywhere she went, Misty made friends. Children and adults alike thought she was the most enchanting, friendly pony they had ever met.

By now, Mrs Henry loved Misty dearly and wanted to keep her for ever but she didn't forget her promise to Grandpa Beebe. While Misty was in her care she wrote several more books about her. A few years later, though, when Misty was old enough to have foals of her own, Mrs Henry returned her to Chincoteague and the Beebe family.

Before Misty left Illinois, many people came to say goodbye to her and wish her luck. Mrs Henry felt sad to see the pony leave but she knew Misty would be happy and contented back in the place where she had been born.

Back on Chincoteague, it soon became clear

that Misty was happy. She galloped through the salt-grass meadows with Grandpa Beebe's other horses and felt the sea wind through her shaggy brown and white coat. Her nostrils flared in the fresh air. This was the place where she had been born. It was where she truly belonged. The wild blood stirred in her veins.

A few months later, the Beebe family's dreams came true and Misty gave birth to her first foal. They named him Phantom Wings for watching Misty galloping so freely along the shore it seemed to them that the pony indeed had wings and could fly. News of the birth was given out on the radio and on the TV. Phantom Wings became as famous as his mother, Misty of Chincoteague.

One day, when Phantom Wings had grown into a fine young colt and Misty was expecting her second foal, a great storm blew up along the coast of Virginia. The inhabitants of the tiny Chincoteague island were used to the storms that raged along the shore but it was soon obvious that this one was worse than most. As the wind increased they secured their windows and doors and prepared themselves for a long and noisy night. Grandpa made sure Misty was safe and secure in her stable before he went to bed. All night long, the storm raged. The wind rattled round the eaves of the Beebes' wooden house and the rain beat a tattoo against the windows. Grandpa still wasn't worried. He had been through many storms in his life and this seemed no worse than most.

But when the family awoke in the morning, to their horror, the sea had risen in the night and was higher than anyone had ever seen it before. The causeway that linked the island to the mainland was under several metres of water. The people of Chincoteague and their animals were completely cut off.

All day the storm continued and the sea rose higher and higher. Then an announcement came over the radio. Everyone had to leave the island; it wasn't safe to stay.

Soon a fleet of helicopters arrived to pick the people up and take them to safety on the mainland. Grandpa and the family didn't want to leave. What would happen to Misty while they were gone? They had already heard that it was feared that many of the wild ponies had been swept away. They couldn't bear it if Misty was lost too.

But the government had ordered people to leave so they had no choice. They waded through the still rising waters and led Misty from her stable to the higher ground where the house stood. They put her in the kitchen, piled hay up on the floor, filled the sink with all the pony food they could find then reluctantly left. Glancing back, they saw Misty gazing at them from the kitchen window with a puzzled look on her face. With aching hearts they wondered if they would ever see her again.

It was almost a week before the waters went down and the residents of Chincoteague were allowed back to their homes. The storm had done a terrible amount of damage. Some houses had been swept away altogether. Some leaned at crazy angles. Some were just piles of matchwood. Boats were skew-whiff on high ground where the gigantic waves had tossed them. The place looked

like a battlefield. The Beebes made their way quickly home with their hearts in their mouths. They dreaded finding Misty drowned, or worse still, disappeared, swept away on the swift currents with no way of knowing if she had lived or died.

But to their great relief, Misty was fine. She had eaten all the food and had even opened the fridge and raided that too. She was looking well and happy to see the family back home. In fact she was so well that, the following day, she successfully gave birth to her second foal. They called it Stormy.

When the mess had been cleared up and things were getting back to normal a wild pony count was held. It was then that the people learned that their worst fears had been realised. Almost half the herd had been lost. It seemed there would never be another round up and carnival in Chincoteague. Everyone felt sad at the loss of the ponies and that their famous yearly event would never be held again.

It wasn't long, though, before someone came up with an idea. Why not buy back the young ponies that had been sold at the last sale? If they could find enough of them they could start a new herd and the wild ponies of Chincoteague and Assateague would be saved. But there was another problem. With all the repairs needed to their homes, the people were broke. There was no money to spare for new ponies.

The storm had been on the news all over the country and many Americans had been wondering about the safety of Misty and the other ponies. The producer of the film about her phoned to ask if she was safe. He was delighted to hear Misty had survived the storms but upset when he heard about the lost ponies. Then he came up with a suggestion. He would send the film round to all the cinemas again and the money taken would go towards buying new ponies. But the mayor of Chincoteague was dubious. Would children want to see the movie again so soon? 'They will if Misty goes with the film,' the producer said. 'Then they'll come, I'm sure.'

And that was how Misty saved the wild pony herd of Assateague. She toured all round the United States of America appearing at cinemas where the film was showing. Stormy went with her and everywhere they went the cinemas were packed. Misty wasn't at all shy. She trotted up on the stage and put her hooves up on her stool so people could shake hands. Everyone loved her good nature and her friendliness. It was as if she knew she had a job to do and was determined to do it well. She was a star all over again.

Misty and Stormy were on tour for three months and by the time they went back to Chincoteague enough money had been raised to buy about fifty ponies. Together, they had saved the herd.

If you went to Assateague today you would still see the wild ponies grazing the windy salt grasses of the island. Among them will be many of the descendants of the herd who had been saved by Misty, the famous wild pony of Chincoteague.

RED RUM
the Record Breaker

On a cold and misty morning at the end of March twenty five years ago, a steeplechase jockey named Brian Fletcher stood by one of the jumps at Aintree racecourse in Liverpool. Brian had gone out early that morning to examine the state of the turf. He was pleased to find it was nice and firm, just right for the horse he was to ride in the important race taking place that day. The race was to be the Grand National, the most famous and gruelling race in the national hunt calendar.

The horse Brian was going to ride in the race was Red Rum, a horse whose name would be on everyone's lips by the end of the day. Brian didn't know then that his mount would win. He didn't know if the horse would even finish the race. Any animal who did manage to negotiate the daunting fences would have to have outstanding courage. In fact, win or not, it would have to be a hero. Brian knew Red Rum was careful, dedicated and braver than any horse he had ever known. He felt confident they could win . . . if they had luck on their side.

What the jockey couldn't have guessed, though, was that Red Rum would not only win that year's Grand National, he would go on to win two more of these tough races and would go down in the record books as the bravest and most determined steeplechaser ever.

Like other famous racehorses before him, Red Rum did not have a very promising start to his racing career, although the problems he had to overcome during his first days in racing showed his owners and trainers the courage he possessed and gave them the faith and hope to carry on. This faith was rewarded beyond their wildest dreams.

Red Rum's story began in 1965 in Ireland when a reddish brown colt was born to a spirited mare named Mared. Mared was an exceptional horse, wild natured and very beautiful. Her owners had hoped she would become a racehorse but she proved too hard to handle. She hated being made to do something she didn't want to do. The young Red Rum soon showed the same kind of spirit. But the colt had more wisdom than his mother. Very early on he decided it was better to enjoy the things you were made to do rather than rebel against them. Luckily for him, though, galloping was the thing he loved best. This and his extreme courage when faced with a challenge would make him a champion.

When Red Rum and the other colts at the stud farm where he had spent his early months were used to being handled they were sold. Red Rum was taken to England to begin his serious training. His days of freedom in the green pastures of Ireland were over.

At that time, Red Rum's new owner didn't realise that this young horse had the potential to become a steeplechaser. His trainers had seen how fast he could run, how he loved to gallop. They decided he would make a good sprinter. Horses who are to race over jumps are usually left until they are about four years of age before their training begins. Red Rum was only two but seemed ready for the racetrack. His trainer's hunch proved to be right and the young horse won five races in quick succession. He seemed to be well on the way to a sprint career when, because of the rules of racing, he was sold again.

At his new stable, Red Rum was unhappy. His old home had been a busy, lively yard with children coming and going and green fields to graze. He was restless and seemed to have made up his mind he would misbehave. But then he was introduced to his new groom and things took a different turn. The groom's name was Sandra and she and Red Rum became friends right from the start. After that he settled down and seemed to be on the way to another round of successes when disaster struck and, for a time, it looked as if the big red horse might never run again.

By now, 'Rummie' as Sandra called him, was jumping over hurdles and she felt very proud of him as she led him into the parade ring before the start of his first jumping race. His coat gleamed red in the sunshine and his muscles rippled beneath his skin. He looked every inch a winner as she handed him over to the jockey who was to ride him that day. But at that moment Rummie seemed to lose his confidence. He had grown used to Sandra on his back and didn't like the strange man who swung his leg over the saddle and quickly gathered up the reins ready for the canter down to the start. The horse could sense there was going to be a battle of wills and his heart sank. Sandra let him do as he liked. She understood how he had to be free to make up his own mind about how fast to run. He had a terrible feeling this time things were going to be different.

Red Rum was soon to realise his fears were coming true. For a start, the ground was too soft and he found the race very hard going. The jockey drove him on against his will and by the end of the course Rummie's love of racing seemed to have dissolved. It was an exhausted and nervous horse who came second that day. Sandra was upset. She thought her beloved horse had been treated badly. She was afraid he would never feel the same about racing again. On the way back to the yard, Rummie glimpsed the fresh green grass of the fields by the side of the road. He could see other horses grazing peacefully in the fresh air and he wanted to join them and not feel the whip on his flank as his jockey urged him forward against his will. By the time they arrived home he was depressed and miserable.

After that, Rummie's spirits were so low that he caught a virus. He didn't win any races that season. No matter how much Sandra tried to cheer him up he couldn't seem to snap out of his depression. It looked as if Red Rum's career was over almost before it had begun. When the season finished he was at last put out to grass. There, at long last, he seemed to recover his spirits. Grazing in the sunshine reminded him of his early days in

Ireland and his strength began to return. Hopes were high for the new season before yet again, disaster struck. Rummie injured his foot and couldn't race for many months. His trainer began to despair – the huge red horse for which he'd had such high hopes was proving to be a walking disaster.

All winter long, Sandra loved and cared for Rummie. She took him out on the gentle exercise the vet had recommended. She fed him the special food to build up his stamina and strength and help heal his injury. The bond between them grew day by day and at last he was fit to race again. His trainer entered him in the Scottish Grand National. He finished fifth.

Sandra was proud of her brave charge and hugged and kissed him when they were back at the yard. He hadn't won but it was his first race for a long time. She knew he had done his best. To her, that was all that mattered. What neither Sandra or Rummie knew was that he had run his last race while in her care. He was to be sold yet again.

When Sandra heard the news, she was devastated. Never again, she thought, would she love and care for a horse so much. It was a sad day for both of them when Red Rum went off to the horse sales. Sandra thought her heart would break as she said goodbye to him for the last time. She hoped he would be happy in his new home, wherever it was. She watched sadly as Rummie was loaded into the horse box and driven away. Through her tears she knew she would always be proud of him. She had loved him for his bravery and for his kindness. Little did she know that in years to come she would have more reason to be proud of Red Rum that she could ever have imagined.

And as for Rummie himself? He was confused and angry at being taken away from his friend. He knew he had done his best for everyone. As he shifted restlessly in his box on the way to the sales he had no idea what the future might hold for him. Everything he had loved and grown used to was being taken away from him. All he had ever wanted was to be allowed to gallop as far and as fast as he liked – to feel the wind through his mane, to run and run. Would his new owner understand that was all he ever wished to do? Only time would tell.

At the sales, Red Rum was bought by a man called Donald McCain. He was bidding on behalf of someone else, Mr Le Mare. Mr McCain understood horses. When he first saw Red Rum he knew he could become a champion steeplechaser. He could see the wild spirit in the horse's eyes. He could see too that Red Rum was upset by the noise and clamour of the horse sale. He put his hand on the animal's neck and spoke to him softly. Red Rum understood how proud Mr McCain was that he had been able to buy him. It seemed a bond of understanding passed between them. Red Rum would do anything to make this man happy. He followed him meekly up into the new horse box and they were on their way to a new home by the sea.

Red Rum soon settled down at Mr McCain's yard. He became part of his family. Mr McCain's wife and children had stared in awe when the horse first arrived. They had other horses but none could compare to this new one. Then, one day, another, older man came to see him. He gazed at the horse with shining eyes. In his smart suit he seemed strangely out of place in the stable yard. He was Mr Le Mare, the man who had put up the money to buy him.

Mr Le Mare stood looking at Red Rum for some time. Then he turned to Mr McCain. 'All my life I've been dreaming about owning a horse that would win the Grand National,' he told him. 'And this is the one that will make my dream come true.'

And this is exactly what Red Rum did. He thrived at his new home. Every day he was taken

to gallop along the beach and bathe his sore leg in the sea. It seemed to be a miracle cure. He had all the freedom of the shore, the sea wind in his face. His dreams were coming true too. The smell of the ocean and the firm sand beneath his hooves seemed to give him a new power and determination. On his training gallops nothing could stop him. Even Mr McCain and his groom, Billy, were amazed how swiftly the horse could run. None of the other horses could keep up with him and when he won his first race for Mr McCain it seemed to be a good omen. He was fast, he was brave and determined. His trainer knew he was ready for the biggest race of his life. The Grand National.

Red Rum's jockey for the race was to be Brian Fletcher. Brian had ridden Rummie before and the horse was very fond of him. The jockey had been delighted when Mr McCain asked him to ride Rummie in his first National. If any horse could win it – Red Rum could!

The Grand National is over seven kilometres long. There are sixteen high fences, fourteen of which have to be jumped twice. That year there were thirty eight runners. Joint favourites were a mighty Australian horse called Crisp and Red Rum. His fame as a galloper had spread and thousands of people turned out to watch him run. As the horses lined up for the start a strange hush came over the crowd. The tension that had been mounting throughout the day seemed to charge the air with electricity. Many people had followed Red Rum's career. They knew he'd had a rocky start to his racing life. They knew he had been unhappy at times and that his determination and courage had overcome many setbacks. Many of them knew too that Red Rum loved to race and a love of racing made a horse a champion. They knew he wouldn't let them down.

Then the starter gave his signal and they were off.

Later, people said there had never been such an exciting National. The joint favourite, Crisp, led for most of the way. While other horses fell or got left behind, Crisp and Red Rum stayed in the lead. Crisp raced on valiantly as the two horses headed up the final slope towards the winning post. Red Rum was a little way behind. The roar from the crowd was deafening. As Red Rum got closer and closer to Crisp he seemed to find a new strength and power. His determination to be first past the post seemed to come from his mind rather than from the sleek, iron-hard muscles of his body. Closer and closer until it was plain that both horses were getting tired. The noise from the crowd swallowed up the thunder of hoofbeats, the drumming of hearts, until with a magnificent last surge of power and determination Red Rum overtook Crisp and went into the lead. He hurtled past the post. In that moment of triumph he turned the dream of his owner's life into reality. Not only had Rummie won his first Grand National, he had broken the course record by covering the ground in the fastest time ever. The crowd went wild with joy.

Red Rum went on to take part in five Grand Nationals altogether. The first one, he won by a short head, his second by a few metres. He came second in the next two and went on to come back and win again when he took part in his fifth. He became an astonishing triple winner of this most difficult and dangerous race. It was a feat never achieved by any horse, before or since. He was truly a record breaker.

In the course of his career, Red Rum made many friends. People loved him for his courage and his character. He knew he was a hero and loved all the adoration he received. His story is a little like a fairy tale. At the beginning everything seemed to go wrong but a happy ending was just around the corner.

Although most of Red Rum's friends were human beings, the horse had another great friend – a donkey called Andy who lived on the farm where the racehorse spent his summer holidays. Andy was generous enough to allow the huge red horse to share his paddock. And when at last the time came for Rummie to finally retire from racing the two animals could often be seen standing together, their faces close, tails gently swishing away the summer insects. It almost seemed as if Red Rum was telling the old donkey about his adventures. He had packed more into his life than most horses, or donkeys, would even dream about.

Even after he had run his last race and taken a unique parade of honour at the Grand National racecourse, Red Rum continued to appear at important events all over the country. He would always be dear to the hearts of the race-going public. Everyone agreed that he deserved every bit of the adoration he so obviously enjoyed. People would never forget him. The magnificent Red Rum – the record breaker!

WITEZ II
the Arabian Prince

It was a warm, spring day when a Californian stud farm owner, Mr Earle Harlbutt, heard some news that was to change his life for ever. There was to be an auction of pedigree horses from the Army Remount Service. The auction was to take place at Fort Reno, Oklahoma and among the horses to be sold was a Polish Arabian stallion named Witez II. Mr Harlbutt felt a quick heartbeat of excitement when he heard the announcement. Ever since he had visited the stallion at the famous Kellogg Arabian Foundation he had longed to own him. He set off for the auction with hope in his heart. If he could manage to buy Witez he would be the happiest man in America.

The story of Witez (pronounced Vee-tezsh) began ten years before and many kilometres away from the United States. As the black clouds of war began to gather over Europe sixty years ago, a dark-bay Arab colt with white blaze and four white socks, was born at the Podlaski State Stud farm in Janow, Poland. This colt, the offspring of two famous Arabians, Ofir, son of a desert-bred stallion and Frederacja, a famous brood mare, was destined to fulfil the prophecy of the name he was given. A name meaning 'chieftain, knight, prince and hero' all rolled into one – Witez. When his registration was returned with 'II' added to the name, his handlers decided there must have been another horse named Witez some years before.

As soon as Witez was born, the young handlers who worked at the stud and who had been chosen to look after him, twins Stasik and Stacia Kowalski, knew he would one day become a famous champion. Not only was Witez the best Arab foal they had ever seen, he had a placid and kindly temperament, unusual in stallions of his breed. As they groomed and petted him he would lay his head against them lovingly. His dark eyes were full of the desert wildness of his ancestors combined with affection for his carers. The twins were proud to have the honour of looking after such a fine animal.

At first, all went well with Witez as he grazed the summer pastures of Janow and it seemed his future was safe and secure. Even when he was accidentally kicked by one of the other young horses and needed emergency surgery he bounced back bravely and suffered no ill effects although he bore the scar above his eye for the rest of his life. A few months later, though, something happened that was to change the young horse's life, from security to danger, from happiness to fear. On September 1st, 1939, when Witez was eighteen months old, Hitler invaded Poland and so began a series of adventures that would lead the horse through many dangerous journeys to the eventual safety of America.

When the Polish handlers learned of the invasion they were desperately afraid. They knew they had to move their beloved horses, to hide them before the troops arrived and took them. The only route open was to the East. They divided the horses into small groups, each travelling with a handler and set off at the dead of night. As Stasik led Witez away from the farm the sky was filled with German bomber planes. The other young horses pranced and whinnied with fear. Only Witez stayed calm. For all of his short life he had put his trust in humans and in spite of the strange thunder in the skies overhead he saw no reason why things should be different now.

But the other young horses were panicked into flight. They scattered in all directions and Stasik and Witez got separated from the others. The young handler's only thought was for the safety of his cherished horse and they pressed on alone. They had to get as far away from the advancing army as they could before it was too late.

But Stasik soon realised they were lost. They had wandered into the marshlands, a bewildering maze of sticky ground. Witez was miserable. He hated mud, it pulled against the muscles of his fine legs and stuck to his dark coat like glue. For every metre of the way he stayed close to Stasik's side until at last they reached solid ground once more. Stasik heaved a sigh of relief. Now, there was another problem. He had to find something to eat for them both. This time, luck was on his side and he came across a group of Polish soldiers who gave them food and shelter. But they warned Stasik – the Nazis were close and they must keep out of their way at all costs.

Witez ate his food gratefully then rested his head on Stasik's shoulder; he badly needed to rest. But there was to be no rest for the two refugees. That night, to everyone's horror, gunfire began cracking through the air. The Nazis had found the camp and were attacking from all sides. Stasik

and Witez fled. They scrambled through the undergrowth and disappeared into the safety of the forest. They could hear German voices, twigs snapping under heavy boots. Suddenly the young man felt a sharp pain in his head. He stumbled blindly on. He had to save Witez even if it cost him his own life. Valiantly, the young horse stayed with his friend until at last they reached a river. Witez drank thirstily as Stasik sank to the ground by his side.

The story of Witez could have ended there if it hadn't been for an old woodsman who found the injured boy and the horse on the banks of the river. He took them to his hut and cared for Stasik until his gunshot wound had healed. So that no-one would be suspicious they harnessed Witez to the woodsman's cart and used him to haul lumber from the forest. Stasik knew if the Germans spotted the valuable horse they would capture him. Russians troops were in the area too. Stasik's heart had turned with fear when he heard. He knew the soldiers must be hungry and there was always the danger that if they took the horse, they would slaughter him for food.

It soon became obvious, though, that Witez could not survive the harsh life of a woodsman's horse. He tried to be brave and did all that was asked of him but Stasik could see his health was failing. The horse needed special food, good quality hay and couldn't live on the meagre rations that were all the old man had to give him. Stasik hatched a plan. He would take Witez back to Janow, hide him away and steal food for him from the farm under cover of darkness. He had to save the horse's life.

When they arrived back at Janow Stasik saw that the stud had been taken over by German soldiers. But they hadn't destroyed it. Many of the escaped Arabians had been recaptured and were being well looked after. The Germans knew and loved good horses and Hitler was using the farm to breed the best horses for the super race of men his crazy mind wanted to create.

Stasik's plan to steal fodder for Witez worked for a while but when things became too hard he made a difficult decision. He had seen the Janow horses were in good health. He realised Witez had a better chance of survival if he took him back there and gave him up to the German veterinary officers who were in charge of the place. With his heart breaking he led Witez back to the farm where he had been born.

At Janow, the German vets were amazed to hear Stasik's story. They petted Witez and, in spite of the traumas he had been through, saw what a magnificent stallion he had become. He still had that princely 'look of eagles' that had inspired his name. They allowed Stasik to stay and care for him. Secretly, Stasik despised the men even though they were kind and loved all the horses. Stasik managed to hide his hatred and counted the blessing that at least Witez was safe.

As the months passed there was a kind of uneasy peace at the Janow farm. Witez grew into the best stallion of his breed that anyone had ever set eyes on. He became a brilliant jumper and was taken briefly to another stud farm in a place called Mlynow. Stasik and one of the other young handlers at Janow, Liselotte, groomed him to perfection when he was due to leave. They watched with pride as Witez calmly entered the truck that was to take him on his journey. Liselotte was afraid the horse would have changed his character by the time he returned. But Stasik reassured her. 'Witez will always be kind,' he said. 'Nothing will change him now.'

Stasik was right. When Witez came back to Janow he was a lot more mature but he was still the good natured, regal horse he had been since the day he was born. On his return he whinnied to them in greeting and blew soft breaths of affection on to their faces.

While Witez had been away, Stasik had joined the partisans working against the Nazis for the freedom of Poland and, a few weeks after the horse's return, their meetings were discovered. Stasik had to flee for his life. Tragically, his sister, Stacia, was killed in the ensuing chase and many Polish people at the farm were arrested. Then came more sad news. Hitler had ordered all the Janow horses to be moved. The British and American troops were advancing on Poland and he wanted 'his' horses to be taken to his 'super stud' farm in a place called Hostau in Czechoslovakia. Liselotte watched Witez go with sadness in her heart. She didn't know what lay ahead for the horse she had loved and cared for. As the rail car carrying Witez passed she called out farewell. Witez answered with the clarion call of the stallion. The sound made her shiver. It was as if Witez knew he would never see his homeland again.

Witez travelled well. After all, train journeys were nothing compared to the hazards he had faced as a yearling in the marshlands and forests of Poland. One of the Janow handlers was with him and he put all his trust in him. He watched the passing countryside, his nostrils flaring to catch new scents. When they reached their destination he leaned his head against the Janow handler's shoulder as if to say goodbye. The man was to return home now the horses had arrived safely at their destination.

At the new farm, Witez was miserable. He grew listless and dull. He missed his friends at Janow. Here, his needs were met but everything was clinical and there was no time for the horse handlers to make friends with their animals. As the year turned, the news came that the Russians were approaching. Their troops had been on the move for months and they were in a desperate state. Once more the horses were in danger of being captured and slaughtered for food. The German vets who had travelled from Janow with the horses began to feel scared. They cared more about their Arabians than anything else in the world. By the time spring arrived they had made a dangerous decision. They would contact the American troops and beg for their mercy. The plan was filled with peril. They must avoid being spotted by their own troops and they had to contact the Americans without getting shot at. If their plan worked, and the Americans agreed to take them, Witez and the other horses would have to face their most dangerous journey yet.

Luck was on the two vets' side as they crept out to meet the American soldiers. They managed to avoid being spotted and when they did arrive at the American camp, the Captain was a horse lover and sympathised with their plight. By now, Witez's fame had spread and many of his foals had gone on to be champions. The Captain knew he had to save him.

In April, 1945 a battalion of American soldiers marched into Hitler's stud farm to rescue the horses. They met with hardly any resistance. They took away the best horses. Amongst them was Witez. The march to the border that followed was over a hundred and fifty kilometres and filled with danger. The line of men and horses was a good target for stray German soldiers haunting the area. Some of the animals were terrified of the gunfire but Witez didn't alter his stride. He had heard it all before.

During the long trek, not a single horse was lost although many became lame as they were unshod. Horse after horse began to hobble along as their hooves wore down and their feet became sore. The vets did what they could to make them comfortable. Men and animals desperately needed a rest but this was impossible. They had to press on. Witez was at the head of the column. He seemed to thrive on the long march, tossing his head and mane and stepping along smartly. He was indeed living up to his name.

At last, safe and sound, they arrived at a place called Monsbach where men and horses could rest. From there they marched into Austria and an American General sent his best horseman to care for them and to make arrangements for them to be transported to America. Then came the news that Hitler was dead and that to everyone's joy and relief, the war was over. The horses were safe at last.

A couple of months later, two people turned up at the farm where the horses were being looked after. One, a young man, was in the uniform of a Polish lieutenant. The other was a dark haired young woman. Stasik and Liselotte had come to be reunited with their beloved stallion, Witez.

When Stasik learned Witez was to be shipped to America, he was furious. 'Will you take our horses as spoils of war?' he asked the Captain angrily. He knew that if Witez had the choice he would want to return to his homeland.

But there was nothing Stasik could do and he comforted himself with the thought that Witez would be safe in America. Safer than in a Poland still full of Russian soldiers. Sadly he said goodbye to his old friend for the very last time. Witez leaned his head against the young soldier's arm. 'Good luck, my Prince,' Stasik whispered. 'Keep safe.'

Liselotte stayed with Witez until, late that summer, he was ready to set off on the longest journey of his life. Witez's years in Europe were over. As the transport ship set sail and the coastline disappeared from view Witez turned his head to face the New World. His eyes seemed to be searching for a fresh challenge. Witez lived for the challenges that he always faced so courageously. A new life in a new country was just another step on the ladder of his success.

After a rough voyage across the North Atlantic the Arabians arrived in Virginia. Many of them had been ill on the journey but Witez was in good condition. His placid temperament had kept him calm during the long voyage. He stayed in Virginia for a short time then travelled to the fabulous Kellogg ranch in Palmona, California, which was then part of the Army stud. It was there that Mr Harlbutt saw Witez for the first time.

The ranch was huge, over eight hundred acres of beautiful rolling countryside. It had been set up by the breakfast cereal millionaire, W.R. Kellogg, for the purpose of raising pure-bred Arabian horses. There were over a hundred stallions there but when Mr Harlbutt saw Witez he knew he was the most beautiful of all. In spite of all his hardships, Witez looked splendid. The world seemed to stop as Mr Harlbutt watched the stallion moving elegantly across the courtyard. His dark coat gleamed in the sun. He turned his fine head and stared at Mr Harlbutt. The man drew in his breath. Witez was the most wonderful example of the breed he had ever seen. And when he was told the stallion had a calm and trusting temperament to go with his good looks, Mr Harlbutt knew that to own Witez would be a dream come true.

The man's dream did come true that day in 1949 at the auction in Fort Reno when he bought Witez II and took him home to Calarabia, his stud farm in California.

Cotton wool clouds drifted lazily in the blue sky as Witez arrived at his new home. He stepped carefully down the ramp of the horse box and sniffed the air. It smelt wonderful. There was a kind man and his wife waiting to greet him. He turned his great, dark eyes towards them then leaned his face against Mr Harlbutt's shoulder. He gave a deep sigh. Witez had travelled a long way to be in that peaceful place. He had been lost in the wild woods of Poland, he had travelled many miles under gunfire, he had been captured by enemy troops, he had been carted from pillar to post. All these memories seemed to fade away as he looked around. These people would give him the love and security he had longed for ever since the day he had been taken away from Janow as a young horse. As he galloped across the wide, green meadows of Calarabia he had never had so much freedom in all of his life. The horse who had belonged to governments and to enemies now truly fulfilled the promise of his name – he became the Prince of Calarabia.

People who loved and admired Arabian horses came from all over the world to see Witez II. He accepted their love and homage with all the gentleness of his fine nature. He won many championships and went on to become the oldest stallion ever to be the American Pacific Coast Supreme Champion. The dreams of his young handlers, Stasik and Stacia were at last fulfilled. Always gentle, always brave, Witez had travelled many kilometres in his lifetime but no-one could ever measure the length of the road that had led him into people's hearts. His trust in the goodness of mankind brought faith and hope to many people caught up in the web of terror and despair of war.

Witez II will never be forgotten. His beauty and grace live on in his many children and in his children's children. They are all proud to call themselves descendants of the famous Witez II – the dazzling, legendary Arabian Prince.

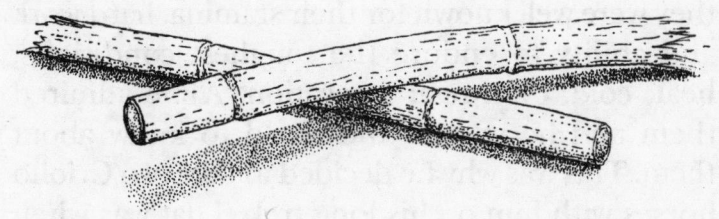

MANCHA AND GATO
heroes of the longest trek ever

Aimé Tschiffely was a man with a secret scheme. For years he had been a schoolteacher, teaching English to children in South America and although his life was pleasant he longed to do something really exciting and different. So Aimé decided he would at last fulfil an ambition he'd had for a long time. He wanted to hike from Buenos Aires in Argentina to Washington in the United States of America. It would be a journey of an amazing sixteen thousand kilometres.

Aimé had another reason for wanting to do this unique journey. He was very fond of horses, particularly the Argentine Criollo horse, a breed that not many people outside of South America knew anything about. In that part of the world they were well known for their stamina, hard work and ability to endure the toughest conditions, heat, cold, even near starvation. Aimé admired them and he wanted the world to know about them. This was why he decided to take two Criollo horses with him on his long trek. That was when Mancha and Gato came into his life.

Criollo horses are descended from horses taken to South America from Spain over four hundred years ago. The Spaniards settled near Buenos Aires but after an attack by the local inhabitants they scattered. Many of their horses were turned loose to survive in the wild and it is from this ancestry that Mancha and Gato came.

The two horses were already sixteen and fifteen years old and had just completed a trek of several hundred kilometres from Patagonia when Aimé met them for the first time. By the usual standards they weren't at all beautiful or elegant. Mancha, the elder of the two, was red with uneven splotches of white, a white face and socks. Gato was a sort of coffee colour, what American cowboys would have called 'buckskin'. They had Roman noses, short, sturdy legs and thick necks. Aimé was to discover that what they lacked in beauty, they made up for in strength and personality. On their two and a half years together he was also to find out that they were the most loyal and willing horses that anyone could ever wish for.

Mancha and Gato had once belonged to a Patagonian Indian chief and were the wildest of the wild. Many attempts had been made to tame them but even when Aimé took them over they were still far from docile. The two were already great pals although Mancha was 'top dog', enterprising and brave. Gato was happy to stay in the background. He was gentle and devoted to his four-hoofed friend. As Aimé was to find out, both were great characters. At different times they could be loveable but infuriating, willing yet stubborn. They were both strong and determined and throughout the journey Aimé discovered they had the kind of stamina that he knew he could not have found in any other breed.

Aimé's first contact with the two horses was when their handler tried to get them into their stables in Buenos Aires. He watched in dismay as they bucked and reared, their hooves clattering on the unfamiliar concrete surface of the yard. These horses were used to wide open spaces, the freedom of the Pampas. They had never seen a town before, let alone a stable. Cars and houses scared them, the noise and hustle and bustle of the city frightened them to death.

When at last the horses had been persuaded to go into the stable, they huddled together for comfort. Aimé wondered what he had let himself in for. Supposing the two horses behaved like this all the time? In fact, throughout the two and a half year journey, Mancha and Gato were never to get used to cars or trucks. They would always rear and plunge whenever they saw one. Aimé would come to dread the approaching sound of an engine on the road because he always knew what was going to happen.

Aimé sighed as he watched Mancha and Gato turn their Roman noses up at the oats and barley they were being offered and begin chomping at the coarse straw bedding. At least, he thought, I'm not going to be bored with these two for company!

In fact, it looked as if all three were in for a very exciting time.

Aimé had chosen South American style riding and pack saddles. He planned to ride one horse while the other carried the luggage. He had spent many months planning ahead. At each town there would be food for the horses and a room for himself. He only hoped that Mancha and Gato would take to strange stables better than the ones prepared for them in Buenos Aires. Time, he decided, would tell.

When the news of Aimé's planned adventure spread, a story appeared in the newspapers. Many people tried to put him off. Such a journey had never been done before. Aimé and the horses would never survive the hardship of the icy mountains, rushing rivers, deserts and forests that they would encounter. Aimé didn't listen. He trusted Mancha and Gato – he was certain they would be able to do it.

After the first thousand kilometres Aimé knew that his faith in his Criollos was going to be well rewarded. They had worked liked heroes. There hadn't been much to eat or drink at times but they were still fit and willing. He rested at a town called Tucuman to build up their strength for the next long leg of the journey. In Tucaman there was a big sugar industry and it was there that the two horses found they had a liking for sugar cane. It seemed to give them extra energy. They would snatch it eagerly from people's hands, munching and crunching until it had all gone.

It took Aimé and his faithful pals a whole year to cross the Andes. They followed the mountain trails as best they could. Through forests, climbing to dizzy heights then clambering down into deep ravines. The countryside was spectacular, Aimé doubted that any traveller had ever had more time to see and understand the people and the wildlife of the countries he crossed. Nor, he thought, did any man ever have two such good friends as he had in Mancha and Gato.

During this part of the journey Aimé hardly met anyone. Those he did encounter had never travelled far from their villages and weren't able to point him in the direction he wanted to go. Often he got lost and had to go back to find the trail again. Once, a cloud of locusts filled the air and the horses were scared. As he reassured them gently, Aimé knew that his two, four-hoofed companions were relying on him as much as he was relying on them. It gave him a feeling of security. Their friendship became his most precious possession.

As man and animals continued their expedition they passed through places where the people had never met a man from the west before. They stared curiously and came to pet the horses. Sometimes he would come across another rider on a shaggy mountain pony and they would pass the time of day. Aimé made the most of these meetings. He would often go for weeks without hearing another human voice.

By the time they reached Bolivia, Aimé was suffering from mountain sickness although the horses showed no ill effects from the high altitude. Aimé was more proud of them than he could say. They were in better condition than when they had started out, hundreds of kilometres back. But they still had a very long way to go. In their path to La Paz, the next stop, lay dangerous ravines, icy rivers and steep, winding trails that would make the most experienced mountaineer dizzy.

Much to Aimé's relief, Mancha and Gato took it all in their stride. They became as sure footed as mountain goats. On the steepest parts of the trails, Aimé would dismount. He would hold on to Mancha's tail and the horse would quite happily haul him up. He didn't mind a bit. Time and again Aimé was filled with pride. His two animal friends were indeed heroes.

After La Paz, the trek took them through the dangerous highlands of Ecuador. Once, the trail had been washed away. On one side was a deep ravine, on the other a high wall. While Aimé tried to decide what to do the horses calmly jumped the yawning gap leaving him to scramble around as best he could. Aimé decided the animals had more courage than he had bargained for. Another time, the ground gave way beneath Gato's feet and he slid down the mountainside, only coming to rest against a tree. He whinnied in fear until Aimé scrambled down to comfort him. Luckily a rider and mule were passing and they helped haul the Criollo back up to the track.

Often, the horses' instincts for danger would save Aimé's life. Once, they refused to go across a piece of land that turned out to be a deep and dangerous bog. Their wild instincts had alerted them. Another time, Aimé had to cling to them for dear life as they crossed a slender hanging bridge slung over a torrential river. He held Mancha's tail while the guide led them to safety. Not once did the horses hesitate as the water rushed beneath the fragile bridge. Again, Aimé was more proud of his horses than ever before.

When the three travellers reached Lima, the capital of Peru, a royal welcome awaited them.

Fine stables, sugar cane and a comfortable bed for Aimé, his first for months. Their fame had spread.

Lots more adventures were to follow and by the time Aimé, Mancha and Gato crossed the equator, they had travelled an amazing seven thousand kilometres. They had spent many weeks trekking across a wild desert region although the horses had hardly ever shown signs of thirst. The worst stretch was at 'Matacaballo', a Spanish word that means 'horse killer'. It took them twenty hours, non-stop. This time the horses did suffer and Aimé was concerned they wouldn't make it. But he need not have worried. Both horses broke into a trot, then a canter as they came close to a river. When they reached the banks, it was in flood and they had to go across with a professional 'horse swimmer'. Again, Aimé feared for their lives but true to their nature the Criollos made it safely to the other side. It would take more than a desert or a raging torrent of water to get the better of Mancha and Gato!

Once across the equator, Aimé celebrated with the best meal that money could buy. Mancha was so fond of sugar cane by now that he escaped from this tether and walked right into a shop that sold it. On their long journey they'd had to put up with many strange foods. Bamboo, yucca, even tobacco leaves, in fact anything they could get their teeth into. But sugar cane was the best of all.

As they tramped on through the rain forests Mancha proved to be a good guard-horse. He would warn of approaching big cats, pumas, jaguars, by neighing loudly and bucking. He would make such a row that the predators would slink away, scared. Then disaster struck. Gato stood on a nail and got a foot infection. It became so painful that people told Aimé he would have to have the horse put to sleep. Aimé wouldn't hear of it and shipped Gato off to Mexico City for treatment. To the man's joy, he recovered well and the three friends were soon back together. Aimé could never have thought about replacing his beloved Gato. He and Mancha were his most trusted friends.

By now, everyone had heard of the epic trek. Aimé, Mancha and Gato were famous. Everywhere they went, people turned out to see them. They would feed tit-bits to the horses and offer Aimé rest and a good meal. Once they reached the large towns of the United States, though, the horses weren't so happy. They missed the open tracks, the rivers and forests. The hard road felt peculiar beneath their hooves and they weren't keen on the strange people that surrounded them wherever they went. They had grown used to one man, their friend Aimé. They also hated the traffic and bewildering mass of buildings. They disliked having to be indoors at night. Aimé had trusted them completely and had turned them loose every evening as he settled down to sleep. He knew they would never stray. Here, they had to be locked up with no stars to light the sky or wind to cool them down. They would nuzzle one another and sigh. Hopefully, when their journey was over, they would be allowed to be free again.

And this is exactly what happened. After a tremendous hero's welcome in every State they passed through the travellers at last arrived in Washington. When the celebrations there were over, Aimé decided the two horses would be returned to the estate from where they had been taken nearly three years earlier. Many people wanted to buy them, to show them off to the public but Aimé refused. He couldn't make an exhibition of his two best friends.

And so after their long trek, Mancha and Gato went home. Aimé went with them on a ship from New York to Buenos Aires. A great crowd turned out to greet them when they arrived. As soon as the parties were over, Aimé took the horses out on to the pampas. As he released their rope halters and they galloped off, happy to be free again he thought of the many adventures they had shared, adventures he could never have had without them. He remembered the dangers they had faced, the warm nights they had spent out under the stars and the trust they had had in one another. Aimé knew he would never forget the bond of love and friendship they had shared.

Aimé was so proud of the horses who had carried him so faithfully, so far, that he wrote a book about their adventures. He called it 'Tschiffely's Ride'. The book told of the wonderful scenery he had seen on his expedition, the remote villages he had visited, the hardships he and the horses had had to overcome, the friends they had made along the way. He had indeed proved that the Criollo horses were the hardiest of all. He had also learned that the bond between a man and his horses is something to be cherished for ever.

As he was writing the book, Aimé's mind would often go back to his four-legged friends, grazing happily and freely on the wild, wind-blown Pampas grasses. They were the true heroes of the story, Mancha and Gato, the Criollo horses who had never once let him down on the journey from Buenos Aires, to Washington – the longest trek ever.

HEROIC HORSES
further reading

You can find out more about the horses in these stories, and other heroic horses too, in these books which might be in your local library or bookshop:

Sefton – The Story of a Cavalry Horse by J.N.P. Watson
(Souvenir Press Ltd)

Misty Of Chincoteague by Marguerite Henry
(Simon & Schuster)

And Miles To Go – The Biography of a Great Arabian Horse by Linell Smith
(Little, Brown and Company)

Tschiffeley's Ride by A.F. Tschiffely
(William Heinemann)

Flyers And Stayers by Margot Lawrence
(George C. Harrap & Co)

Red Rum – Born to Win: The Story of Red Rum by Christine Pemberton
(Hodder & Stoughton)

TRUE ANIMAL STORIES
Devoted Dogs

Sue Welford

Meet Rats, *the hardy army dog whose courage helped soldiers survive the toughest of times* . . . Micky, *the digger dog who didn't believe his best friend was dead* . . . Cinnamon, *the earthquake dog – her job was to save lives* . . .

Including the classic tales of Greyfriars Bobby and Gelert, who gave his life for a prince, here are eleven heart-warming stories of dogs whose devotion proved they really were man's – and woman's – best friend!

JESS THE BORDER COLLIE 1
The Arrival

Lucy Daniels

Jess the Border collie puppy owes his life to Jenny Miles, and he'd do anything for her. They're the best of friends and, together, they're ready for all sorts of adventures!

Jenny lives with her family on a busy sheep farm in the Scottish Borders. Life is hard on the farm – and money is always tight. Even a new puppy has to earn its keep. So when Nell the sheepdog gives birth to a tiny puppy with a twisted leg, his future looks bleak. But Jenny sees that even though Jess will never be a working dog, there is something very special about him . . .

Another Hodder Children's book

JESS THE BORDER COLLIE 2
The Challenge

Lucy Daniels

Jess the Border collie puppy owes his life to Jenny Miles, and he'd do anything for her. They're the best of friends and, together, they're ready for all sorts of adventures!

It's lambing season at the farm, and this year there are more orphaned lambs than ever. Without more help to feed them, there's a danger that many of the lambs will die.

Jenny sees how gentle Jess is with the tiny lambs – perhaps there's a way he can help . . . ?

ORDER FORM

Sue Welford

0 340 74421 9   TRUE ANIMAL STORIES: *DEVOTED DOGS*   £3.99 ❐

Lucy Daniels

0 340 70438 1   JESS THE BORDER COLLIE 1: *THE ARRIVAL*   £3.99 ❐
0 340 70439 x   JESS THE BORDER COLLIE 2: *THE CHALLENGE*   £3.99 ❐
0 340 70440 3   JESS THE BORDER COLLIE 3: *THE RUNAWAY*   £3.99 ❐

All Hodder Children's books are available at your local bookshop, or can be ordered direct from the publisher. Just tick the titles you would like and complete the details below. Prices and availability are subject to change without prior notice.

Please enclose a cheque or postal order made payable to *Bookpoint Ltd*, and send to: Hodder Children's Books, 39 Milton Park, Abingdon, OXON OX14 4TD, UK.
Email Address: orders@bookpoint.co.uk

If you would prefer to pay by credit card, our call centre team would be delighted to take your order by telephone. Our direct line *01235 400414* (lines open 9.00 am–6.00 pm Monday to Saturday, 24 hour message answering service). Alternatively you can send a fax on *01235 400454.*

TITLE		FIRST NAME		SURNAME	

ADDRESS	
DAYTIME TEL:		POST CODE	

If you would prefer to pay by credit card, please complete:
Please debit my Visa/Access/Diner's Card/American Express (delete as applicable) card no:

Signature .... Expiry Date: ....

If you would NOT like to receive further information on our products please tick the box. ❐